EVERGREEN

MORE FOLK TALES FROM AROUND THE WORLD

© Shree Book Centre

More Folk Tales from around the world
ISBN : 978-81-7963-261-1

Reprinted in 2013

© Shree Book Centre

Printed in India

All rights reserved. No part of this publication may be reproduced or transmitted in any form or by any means, electronic or mechanical, including photocopying, recording, or by any information storage and retrieval system, without permission in writing from the publishers.

Published by

SHREE BOOK CENTRE
8, Kakad Industrial Estate, S. Keer Marg
Off L.J. Road, Matunga (W)
Mumbai - 400016 (India)
Tel : 91-22-24377516 / 24374559
Telefax: 91-22-24309183
E-mail: sales@shreebookcentre.com

CONTENTS

1. Sands of Gold — 5
2. Ivan and the Grey Wolf — 9
3. The Adventurous Youth — 16
4. An Ill-tempered Bride — 21
5. The Clever Deer — 28
6. The Clever Lad and his Six Men Army — 32
7. The Clever Rabbit — 39
8. Most Mystical Pot — 45
9. An Enchanted Bottle — 51
10. Four Magic Bowls — 58
11. The Golden Shoes — 64
12. The Kind-hearted Old Man — 73
13. A Little Warrior — 81
14. The Mermaid Who Loved Music — 87
15. The Miller Who Turned Into a Donkey — 94
16. The Paintbrush Phenomena — 101
17. The Mountain Spirit — 106
18. The Two Bachelors and a Python — 111
19. The Woodcutter and his Enchanted Pitcher — 116
20. When the Coyote Stole Fire — 123

Sands of Gold

A Nepalese Folk Tale

The ruler of Bhadgao in Nepal was once told a curious thing by the court astrologer. "Your majesty, if you collect the sand from the shores of Lakhu at a certain auspicious time, then it'll turn into gold after 12 hours!"

The king was impressed. He immediately sent two labourers to collect the sand. They reached the pilgrim centre of Lakhu that was located where the rivers Bhatikhu and Vishnumati met. And at the specified time they filled their baskets with sand and started their journey back.

When they reached Kathmandu, a sand merchant named, Sakhwal saw them. "I shall pay you handsomely for your sand," he offered. The labourers saw a good opportunity and agreed. "After all we can always go back and collect more sand," they decided. And they returned to collect more sand for the King, but alas, it was not the auspicious time!

And so, after the specified time the king's sand remained unchanged while Sakhwal's sand shone and glittered. 'Golden sand! I've never seen anything like this!' thought Sakhwal. But he wasn't sure if the gold was rightfully his.

He decided to ponder over it while taking a walk. As he walked he overheard a conversation between a moneylender and a poor peasant. "Pay up now or give me your house!" demanded the moneylender. "Please, sir, give me another month!" pleaded the peasant. But the moneylender was unmoved.

Touched by the plight of the poor man, Sakhwal entered the moneylender's shop and thrust a bag of gold at him. "Here, keep this! And do not harass this poor man any more!" "I can't take gold from an untouchable!" said the moneylender for Sakhwal was of low caste. "My gold is not untouchable, only I am" replied he and left. The poor man turned to thank him but he was gone.

As Sakhwal walked on he thought, 'There are so many like that poor man, who need help. I should help them out with the gold I have.' He went to the King, Jayadeva Malla. "Greetings, Maharaja!" he said. "Greetings!

What is it you came for?" asked the king. "I happened to buy some sand that turned into gold. And since I do not deserve such wealth I thought I could put it to good cause," said Sakhwal. "Well, what would you like to do with it?" asked the king, amused.

"I'd like to free all poor people who are in the clutches of the evil moneylenders. And I came here to seek your permission," he announced. The king was moved. "You're a noble and generous man. I salute you!" And Sakhwal was named as Shankhdhar after Lord Vishnu, the divine protector.

"And to remember this wonderful gesture, the calendar we follow shall be called Shankhdhar Samvat from now on. And today shall be the first day of that calendar," declared the king. And that's the calendar followed in Nepal even today.

Sakhwal started his good work and saved many from the misery of debt. Each poor man went away blessing him and praising him to the skies. A statue of him stands at the southern gate of the famous Pashupathinath temple in Nepal!

Ivan And The Grey Wolf
A Russian Folk Tale

There once was a tsar who had three handsome sons. The last, Tsarevich Ivan was their father's favourite. The tsar had the most beautiful garden, an exotic apple tree which sprouted golden apples! Once someone started stealing the golden apples from the tree. The tsar was terribly upset that none of his soldiers could find the thief.

Finally the tsar asked his sons to help. The first son stood guard on the first night. But soon he fell asleep and when he opened his eyes it was dawn and an apple had been stolen. The second son failed as well.

Then it was Ivan's turn. At midnight he saw the most astonishing sight. A lovely golden bird descended from the sky and perched on the apple tree. It shimmered and glittered like fire for it was the Fire Bird!

Ivan pounced on it but it was too quick for him. It flew away and Ivan was left with a golden feather. He ran to his father who was very pleased with him.

"Ivan, you've made me proud. This bird

sounds very unique. We must have it!" and he sent his three sons to find it and bring it back.

The three set off in three directions. As Ivan rested by the wayside, a big grey wolf appeared, pounced on his horse and ran away with it. Deprived of his horse Ivan walked and walked for days until he was too weary for words. He sat down under a tree in despair. Suddenly the grey wolf came before him. "Why are you sad?" he asked Ivan. Ivan told him his mission. "Well, my lad, that's no easy task. But I shall help you, so jump on my back!"

And they were off like the wind. The wolf seemed to be flying and very soon they were outside a palace. "Go over the palace wall into the garden. There sits the Fire Bird in a golden cage. Just take the bird, don't touch the cage!" instructed the wolf.

Ivan did as he was told and found the bird. "But what a beautiful cage – I can't leave it behind!" and he picked up the cage. At once the trumpets sounded and an army of soldiers ran towards him and dragged him to the tsar of that land.

Ivan And The Grey Wolf

"If you want me to spare your life," thundered the tsar. "Go, fetch me a horse with the Golden Mane. Then I shall give you the Fire Bird!"

Ivan and the Wolf set off again. Soon they reached another castle and the wolf instructed him to go over the wall into the stable and lead the horse out. "But don't touch the bridle!"

When Ivan saw the horse he was enchanted, for it had a glittering golden mane. But he could not resist picking up the beautiful golden bridle. Instantly the trumpets blared, soldiers came running and he was dragged off to the tsar. This tsar threatened Ivan with death.

"But I shall give you one more chance. Bring me Elena, the Fairy and you can have my horse. Koshchei, the deathless holds her prisoner. Succeed if you can or die trying! Ha, ha!" rollicked the tsar.

And Ivan and the Wolf set off once more until they reached a forest. "Find the witch, Baba Yaga and ask her where you can find the Life of Koshchei," tipped the Wolf and

Ivan And The Grey Wolf

disappeared. Ivan walked on until he came to the hut of Baba Yaga, who helped him because he was a friend of the Grey Wolf. "The Life of Koshchei lies in an egg in the middle of an island," she divulged to Ivan.

After many more adventures, Ivan finally got the egg and set off for Koschei's castle. At the gate he battled a twelve-headed dragon with great courage and entered the castle. When he saw Elena, the Fairy he was mesmerised. For never had he seen such beauty and radiance!

Elena looked up and saw her saviour and instantly fell in love with the handsome young man. As they stood gazing at each other, Koshchei, the deathless entered the chamber and roared with fury. In a second, Ivan took out the egg and smashed it onto the ground. Koshchei went up in smoke! Elena, the Fairy was free at last!

Going back to the tsar who owned the Golden maned horse they reunited with the Wolf who offered a hide. When they reached the castle, Elena and Ivan did not have the heart to part.

More Folk Tales From Around The World

And so the Wolf rolled on the ground and in a minute he had taken the form of Elena! Ivan led him in and the tsar was overjoyed. Taking the Golden Maned horse, Ivan left with the real Elena.

Soon after, the tsar discovered that his bride was a wolf and became furious. But it was too late. The Wolf escaped too and caught up with the others.

Now Ivan hated to see his lovely horse go to the other evil tsar. So the Wolf took the form of Golden Maned horse and Ivan led him in. In two days, the tsar rode on his magnificent horse, only to be knocked off when it turned into a wolf and ran away!

Now they were almost near home, when Ivan and Elena parted ways with the Wolf. They decided to take a nap. As they slept, Ivan's older brothers who were returning home with nothing, spotted them.

"Look, he has the Fire Bird! And a beautiful maiden and a Golden Maned horse!" they exclaimed.

Ivan And The Grey Wolf

The evil brothers killed him quietly and dragged the other three home, threatening Elena with death if she said anything.

Soon the Grey Wolf came and saw Ivan dead. He quickly revived him with Water of the Living. The two rushed home for the older son who was about to wed Elena that day.

In the meantime, everyone at the castle was miserable. Elena wouldn't stop crying, the Fire Bird never sang and the Horse with the Golden Mane never ate. The moment they saw Ivan everything changed. The Fire Bird burst into a song. The horse neighed in delight and started to eat. And Elena's face brightened into a radiant smile and she rushed to embrace Ivan.

The tsar was furious with his older sons, but Ivan forgave them and set them free. Ivan and Elena were then married and lived very happily at the palace. And the Grey Wolf stayed on to help Ivan when he became the tsar.

The Adventurous Youth

A Native American Folk Tale

There was once a young man who longed for great adventures. And so he set off from home one fine day. "I shall not return until I've had some wonderful experiences," he declared.

He encountered many things until at last he came to a village at the edge of a forest. As he was about to enter he looked up and saw a lovely young woman sitting on one of the lower branches of a tree, sewing.

'Oh, she is beautiful,' he thought, awestruck. Instead of entering the village he walked past her and then walked back again, passing the tree many times. And each time his love grew more and more.

For days he wandered near the forest, without entering the village. And every day he saw the girl. At last, one day he mustered some courage and approached her.

"I've been watching you for days now and have fallen in love with you. Will you be my wife?" he asked.

The Adventurous Youth

The girl blushed. "I'd love to, but my grandmother does not want me to marry. She's a wicked old lady and has killed many men who had asked for my hand in marriage."

"Hmm. In that case, we shall run away," said the young man. And so they planned that when the grandmother slept that night she'd sneak out and elope with him.

And so at nightfall the girl crept out and they fled. By morning they were very far away. But the girl kept looking nervously over her shoulders.

"What are you afraid of? We are too far away to be caught!" assured he.

"Oh, but my grandmother knows some powerful magic and can cover this entire journey with one leap! I sense that she's right behind us," said the shaky girl.

"Well, don't worry, for I know some magic too," comforted the young man. He threw down his mitten and the road became the trail of a buffalo. And when he threw down the other mitten there was a carcass of a buffalo lying across it.

"She won't get past this," he said.

But the girl continued to look behind as they ran. And in no time they saw the old woman closing in on them with her long strides.

The girl removed her comb from her hair and tossed it behind them. Instantly, a dense forest grew and the old woman could not get past it!

However, with difficulty she escaped and continued to chase them. When she nearly caught up with the lovers, the girl threw an awl (a kind of tool) behind her and instantly a high range of mountains appeared. It had the highest peaks and steepest cliffs and the old woman found it harder than ever to climb.

But her magic was strong too and she managed to cross it and chased them. In the meantime the two had reached a river. "Oh, how do we cross? There's no boat or bridge," cried the girl in panic.

Two cranes were standing in the water. "My friends, can each of you stand on the

banks opposite and stretch your necks so that we can cross?" asked the young man.

The cranes agreed and the two crossed over. "Thank you! And if an old woman happens to come here and asks you to help her across, just pretend to help her. But when she's halfway through, drop her into the water," requested the young man.

Very soon the old woman reached the river. Already fuming at how the two had outwitted her, she screamed at the cranes. "Come here, you stupid ugly birds and help me across the river!"

The two cranes stood beak to beak, and when she was halfway across their beaks, they pulled apart. Alas! Down she went with a splash and was swept away in the raging torrent of the river's strong currents. She quickly got drowned for the magic could not save her from water.

And the young man and his lovely bride returned home and got married in a great ceremony.

An Ill-tempered Bride

An Arabian Folk Tale

There was once a young man named Yunus who was looking for a bride. One day when he glanced out of his window, he saw at his neighbour's window, a very pretty girl.

'Ah! If only she could be my wife!' he longed for.

Every day he'd see her and his yearning increased. One day he went to see his neighbour. "Do you have any objection to my marrying your daughter?" he asked the girl's father.

"Oh, not at all! But there's a small problem," replied the neighbour.

"What's it?" asked Yunus.

"You see, my daughter has the worst temperament you ever saw. No one can spend a minute in her company without getting vexed. I don't want you to get entangled to that kind of a wife," said the man.

"Oh, but she looks so sweet-tempered," said Yunus.

More Folk Tales From Around The World

"Misleading, my friend. But there's one way. Three drops from the Well of Sweetness will cure her of her terrible temper," said the father.

"And where do I find it?" asked Yunus.

"An old beggar woman outside the mosque knows."

At once Yunus went to the mosque and asked the old woman.

"Travel to the west for seven days and then to the east for seven more. You'll come to a river. When you cross it you will reach the country of a giant. He'll tell you," said she.

Yunus walked on up to the river where a boatman waited to ferry people across. "Do you know where the giant lives?" asked Yunus.

"He lives in a cave up in the mountains. Remember to be polite to him or he'll kill you," cautioned the boatman.

Yunus trudged up the mountain until

An Ill-tempered Bride

he reached the cave. He bowed low to the giant.

"Greetings, oh noble giant!" he said politely, "I seek your help in finding the Well of Sweetness!"

The giant was pleased with him. "Had you been rude I would've crushed you with my club."

He, then told him how to get to his destination. "There's a secret passage in this cave and it is guarded by a three-headed dragon. When you get near him, say, 'By leave of Suliman, let me pass!' and he shall let you through to the well."

And Yunus set off until he came to the dragon. It was breathing fire and lashing its tail viciously. When it saw Yunus it got ready to burn him to ashes. Yunus hastily yelled, "By leave of Suliman, let me pass!"

And the dragon did not breathe fire on him and let him pass without harming him. He walked a very long way until suddenly he saw a bright light in the distance. As he

An Ill-tempered Bride

neared it, he saw a beautiful fairy drawing water from a well.

"Greetings, beautiful fairy!"

"Greetings, mortal. What can I do for you?" asked the enchanted creature in a sweet voice.

"I wish for three drops from that well," replied Yunus.

And so the fairy took the pot he had with him and filled it with water from the Well of Sweetness.

Delighted, Yunus thanked her and ran back. Once again he uttered the magic words to the dragon, which let him pass through.

When he reached the giant he encountered a problem. "I've done you a favour, now you must repay it," demanded the giant.

"What must I do?" asked Yunus.

"You must be my slave for a year and a day," concluded the giant.

More Folk Tales From Around The World

Although he was dismayed he had no choice. He toiled hard for the giant, cutting grass for his goats, milking them every day, cooking the giant's meals, washing his clothes and dishes and so on. Soon a year and a day had passed by and he took leave of the giant.

"You've been a good slave. Here, take this bag of gold and be happy," said the giant.

Yunus returned home and went to his neighbour's house. "I'm back with what you've asked for," he disclosed.

"I wondered why you were away so long. I thought I sent you into danger and you would not return," said the neighbour. "Now, let me give my daughter the magic drops so you both can get married."

The wedding day dawned and Yunus got dressed in all his finery. Amidst great pomp and ceremony the wedding took place.

On their wedding night the beautiful bride entered Yunus' room. As his wife spoke to him in a sweet, lovely voice, Yunus heaved a sigh of relief.

An Ill-tempered Bride

"My dear wife, I'm so happy that the Well of Sweetness has helped you or else I might not have been this happy to hear your voice," he smiled.

"What are you talking about? My voice has always been this way," said his wife.

"But your father..." said the puzzled Yunus, "He told me that you were terribly bad tempered and needed a cure from the Well of Sweetness."

The girl burst out laughing. "Oh, he has duped you! It's not me but my mother who has a terrible temper. My father has suffered for years due to her sharp, nasty tongue and was longing for a release. You were the scapegoat!"

Poor Yunus! But what could he do but to laugh? "Ha, ha! At least I shall have a good tempered mother-in-law!"

And they lived in peace for the rest of their lives.

The Clever Deer

A Malaysian Folk Tale

There was once a very clever Mouse Deer. It is a kind of a small deer with no antlers. He was a cheerful young thing and hopped around, singing all day. One day he walked through the forest looking for tasty fruits and roots to eat. Suddenly he heard a loud growl! It was a tiger.

'Oh my goodness! I am done for! I shall surely be eaten now!' thought mouse deer. "Aha! Caught you!" said tiger triumphantly. 'Just as I was getting hungry too!' the Mouse deer thought fast. "I cannot be your lunch tiger. I'm so sorry!" "Why not?" thundered the tiger. "I've been sent by the king to guard his delicious pudding!" lied he. "Where's it?" asked the tiger eagerly. "Why, there of course, by the tree," indicated the deer.

The tiger looked and there was a pool of mud there. "It looks yummy! Can I have a bite?" he asked, his mouth watering. "No, no! I shall be sentenced to death! It's the King's pudding!" said the deer in mock horror. "Oh

More Folk Tales From Around The World

please! Just a small bite. No one will ever know!" pleaded tiger. "Well, all right, but wait till I go far away so no one can blame me!" said the Mouse Deer.

The tiger agreed and the Mouse Deer ran for his life. The tiger ran to the puddle and took an eager sip. "Yeeooooow", he cried spitting out the mud in disgust. "I've been tricked. This's just mud!" And he sprang after the Mouse Deer and soon found him. "You rascal! You've tricked me! But you are caught this time! I shall eat you now!"

"Oh, you can't!" said the Mouse Deer. "The King asked me to guard his drum!" "What drum?" asked the foolish animal. "It hangs from the tree and makes the most wonderful sound you have ever heard," said the Mouse Deer slyly. It was a wasp's nest. "Oh, please let me beat it!" asked the tiger. "The king would kill me!" said Mouse Deer. And so they argued until the tiger agreed to beat the drum after the deer went far away.

The moment the tiger hit the wasps' nest with his paws, hundreds of wasps

The Clever Deer

swarmed around him stinging him viciously. "Ooooooooowww!" he howled running blindly until he reached a stream. He quickly jumped in and saved himself. This time he was furious. "That stupid deer. I shall hunt him down and throttle him!" and he sprang out. He soon caught up with the Mouse Deer. "You shall die at my hands!"

"No, no! I'm guarding the king's belt!" said the Mouse Deer, pointing to a huge python curled up under a tree. "Ha! I shall take it and get you in trouble," said the stupid tiger.

And he picked up the sleeping python and started tying it around his waist. He did not have to finish, for the angry python immediately wound himself around the tiger and squeezed him harder and harder until he could breathe no more!

And the clever Mouse Deer skipped away singing happily. He never had to fear that tiger again.

The Clever Lad and his Six Men Army

A French Folk Tale

In a corner of France was a kingdom whose ruler had a lovely daughter. But he did not want to get her married off for he loved her dearly and wanted her with him all the time.

'Besides, no one can match her beauty or brains,' he thought.

But everyone around him nagged him and pestered him until he came up with a plan. "All right! I shall get her married to the man who can build a ship that sails on land and water!" he declared, thinking it was an impossible task.

News of this challenge spread far and wide until it reached the ears of two brothers in a little village. The older brother was very clever with his hands and could make anything.

"I shall win the princess," he told his younger brother. He set off with his tools to the forest to cut down trees and build a ship.

Along the way he came across an old woman.

"Greetings to you, young carpenter," she said.

But he was rude to her and ignored her greeting.

"Where are you off to?" she asked.

Annoyed, he replied, "I'm going to make skittles with my tools."

"Very well, skittles they shall be then!" she said.

Soon he got to work, chopping wood. But everything he shaped, carved or felled turned into skittles! He tried and tried and spent the whole day working. But still he got only more skittles.

Fuming with rage he finally gave up and went home. "It was foolish to think of building a boat like that! No one can do it!" he told his brother.

"I shall try my hand tomorrow," said the younger one and he took his tool-box and

The Clever Lad and his Six Man Army

reached the forest the next morning.

"Greetings young lad! Where are you off to?" asked the old woman who was at the same spot.

"Greetings to you, too!" he returned and told her his task.

"You shall succeed. And once the ship is ready you will meet six men – take them along to help you," she advised.

And the young man set to work. He only had to chop trees and every piece of wood shaped itself and fell into place. Soon a majestic ship was ready and it could sail on land and water!

He got in and sailed towards the castle until he came across a man who was lying on his stomach by the river. When someone wanted to cross the river he would swallow the whole river in one gulp so they could get to the other side.

"Come with me to the king!" cried the young lad. And the man joined him.

Further down, they saw another man with a very large mouth who was chewing up a mountain. "Come with me to the king!" said the lad and the man joined the two.

Soon they came across the third man who was blowing so hard that he could turn windmills that were miles away. He joined the group, too.

As they travelled they saw the fourth man with very large ears, lying on the ground and listening to the sound of caterpillars underground. He had the sharpest ears in the world. Soon he was part of the group.

They came across two more men who joined them as well. Of these two the first could throw stones from miles away and hit his target accurately. The last had the longest legs ever and could run faster than a hare!

And so the whole lot of them sailed in the ship to the castle. The king was dismayed.

"Before you marry my daughter, you have another task to do," he said. "I need someone to drink all the wine in my cellar for it has gone sour."

At once, the River-drinker was called forth and in a minute, he drank even the last drop of wine from the rows and rows of barrels! The king was shocked!

"Oh, but there's still a lot of stale bread that I cannot serve at your wedding. That has to be finished, too!"

And the Mountain-eater came up and ate every last piece of bread from the big pile.

"My castle lies a little too much in the shade. One of you must turn it towards the sun," demanded the desperate king.

The Wind Blower was called and he blew so hard that the castle turned towards the sun in a short while!

The king then went to the tallest tower in his castle and whispered in his daughter's ears, "Go to the treasure tower deep in the mountains and get the wedding jewels." The princess rode off in the swiftest horse.

Sharp-ears had heard every word they spoke. When the king asked them to find the princess and bring her back, the lad called Long-legs. "Go, bring her back," he said.

And Long-legs covered the journey in a few strides and caught up with her. The clever princess stopped. "I shall rest now," and she sat under a tree. Long-legs rested too but he soon dozed off. In a jiffy the princess mounted her horse and rode off.

Now Sharp-ears heard the snores of Long-legs and told the lad. "Quick, Stone-thrower, wake up Long-legs," cried the lad.

Stone Thrower drew back his arm and hurled a stone that hit Long-legs on the nose. Jumping up, Long-legs raced after the princess and brought her back to the castle.

Now the king had no choice but to give the young lad his daughter's hand in marriage. And so the couple lived happily ever after and the six men army was always there to help them out.

The Clever Rabbit

An African Folk Tale

Kalulu was a rabbit living in the forests of Africa. One day while he rested under the trees he saw some monkeys playing. One monkey reached out his tail and caught his brother round the neck. The helpless brother hung in mid-air and was unable to free himself.

'That's so clever!' thought the rabbit. 'I shall try it too.'

Kalulu had no long tail so he hunted for forest creepers. When he had enough he wound them into a noose. This he hung on a branch of a tree with the noose in mid air.

For days he caught small animals like this who escaped only with great difficulty. 'Ha, ha! I can trick anyone,' thought Kalulu. And no one ever suspected that a rabbit was behind this. They all thought it was an accident.

One day Polo, the elephant decided to build a new village. "Come, all my friends. Help me build a new place to live!"

More Folk Tales From Around The World

All the animals gathered to help him except for Kalulu. He had been distracted by the delicious smell of beans that came from Polo's house. 'Oh I must have some of those beans! My mouth is watering!' thought Kalulu. He waited till the beans were cooked and cooled.

Then he sprang out from behind a bush and ate every one of the beans. Polo returned home after a hard day's work and was furious to see his dinner gone. "Who dared to eat my food?" he raged. But no one could answer.

The next day Polo called Ntambo, the lion. "You lie in wait behind a bush and catch the thief who comes for my food," he instructed.

But Kalulu had overheard the plan and so he spent the whole night making a noose. The next day he arranged the noose in a path close to Polo's cooking pots.

The next morning all the animals left for work and Kalulu casually strolled out into the open and began to eat Polo's beans. He could see the lion hiding.

The Clever Rabbit

The lion bided his time and suddenly sprang out. But Kalulu was prepared for him. He was off like a shot and went along the path where the noose was. The lion chased him. Kalulu sprang through the noose and when the lion tried he was caught in it and swung in the air!

There he struggled and struggled until evening when the other animals returned. "Oh, what happened?" they cried.

"It was an accident," said Ntambo. For he was too ashamed to say it was a mere rabbit that had outwitted him.

Polo then assigned the task of catching the thief to the buffalo, Mbo. This time Kalulu had swung a noose between two palm trees.

Kalulu ate the beans and when Mbo started to chase him, he ran in between the two trees and the buffalo followed. The next instant he was caught by the noose and hung there in mid-air. He kept wriggling there till evening when the other animals set him free.

"It was an accident!" said the buffalo for

The Clever Rabbit

he was sure they would mock him for having been tricked by a rabbit.

And the rabbit went on to trick the leopard, the boar, the dog and other animals. Every day poor Polo's lunch was stolen!

Finally one day Nkuvu, the tortoise went to Polo. "I shall help you catch the thief. He is too wily and I think I can catch him."

The next morning Nkuvu asked Polo to smear him with salt and put him inside the plate of beans. And so it was done and Nkuvu hid amidst the beans.

Kalulu as usual set up his noose and skipped along to have his meal. 'Oh the beans are nicer than ever today – so salty and tasty!' he thought as he gobbled. But when he was halfway through, Nkuvu clamped his mouth around Kalulu's leg and wouldn't let go.

"Ooowwwww," cried the rabbit in pain, "Let go of me, let go of me."

The tortoise retained his tight grip. Kalulu begged and pleaded. But Nkuvu said nothing.

Kalulu threatened and bribed. But nothing worked.

At last it was evening and all the animals returned. "Ah so it is you Kalulu! Clever Nkuvu has caught you!" said Polo.

Now, all the animals discussed how to punish Kalulu. "I think he has to be treated the same way he treated us," said the lion.

And so they hung him up with his own noose for six full days. Every day they would hang him and go to work leaving Kalulu hanging. With no food or water for so many days, the rabbit became thin and frail.

Finally, the others took pity on him and set him free. "Remember, it is better to work for food than to steal it," advised the tortoise.

And the rabbit never stole again nor did he use his noose again on any animal.

Most Mystical Pot

A Czech Folk Tale

There once lived a widow and her daughter. They were desperately poor and just about managed to get by. The only way they survived was with the help of their hens whose eggs they sold in the market. The old woman would go into the forest and pick strawberries out of which they made gruel to eat.

One day the mother fell ill. "You must go to the forest by yourself today," said the woman. And so the girl set off with a basket for strawberries and some bread for lunch. She picked strawberries until her basket filled up, then sat down to her lunch. Just as she was about to eat, an old woman came hobbling up. She had an old pot in her hand and she looked like a beggar.

"My dear child, do you have anything to give an old hungry woman?" she asked. The kind-hearted girl at once handed her bread to the old woman. "Here, eat this. I only hope the old bread is not hard for you to chew."

The woman ate every morsel gratefully. When she had finished she said, "You're a good, kind person. And you shall be rewarded for it." And the old woman gave her pot to the girl. "Oh, please don't give me your pot – surely you need it! Besides, we have pots at home," said the girl.

"My dear, this is no ordinary pot. Just set it down and say, 'Cook, Pot' and it will cook you the most delicious gruel you ever ate. And once it has cooked enough to fill your stomach say, 'Stop, pot' and it will stop," explained the old woman, who wasn't a beggar after all.

The overjoyed girl thanked her profusely and ran home to her mother. "Mother, look! We shall never go hungry ever again!" and she narrated the whole story. Although she was happy, the widow was a little worried as well. "It's a magic pot and sometimes magic turns against you," she said. "Oh rubbish!" scoffed the girl. "Come, let us try it right away."

And so they set the pot on the table and the girl said, "Cook, Pot". The pot started to cook the most delicious-looking gruel. When

it had reached the brim she said, "Stop, Pot" and it stopped at once. The two sat down to a hearty meal and loved every spoon they ate. At last they sat back, contented.

The next morning they had some more of the gruel and the girl said, "All right, mother. I shall take off for the market now to sell eggs." The girl went to town and was delayed at the market. Her mother waited and waited all day for her but she didn't return. By evening she was starving. 'Oh, when will she come? I shall die of hunger. Perhaps I should try out the pot myself,' thought the mother. She placed the pot on the table and said, "Cook, Pot". The pot started cooking merrily.

"I shall go get my bowl and spoon," said the woman to herself and went inside the kitchen. When she returned she was taken aback. The pot had cooked so much gruel that it overflowed from the pot and ran all over the table. "Don't cook, don't cook, stop!" cried the woman. But these weren't the right words and so the pot cooked on and on! "Oh, what are the magic words?" said the woman in panic, 'How do I stop this?"

Most Mystical Pot

The pot cooked more gruel until it ran down from the table and on the floor. Soon the whole kitchen was flooded with gruel. "I knew we should not use magical things!" wailed the woman, jumping up on a chair.

And still the pot cooked while the gruel flowed outside the house and into the streets. Passers-by were shocked. "Oh, what is that? Is that lava flowing down our roads?" cried the stunned people.

The gruel now flowed down the streets and into shops and houses. People struggled to climb up to their top floors. And those who couldn't, jumped up onto chairs and tables.

The pot still kept cooking. Children had a good time though. They stood on high platforms and with little cups, scooped up gruel from the roads and ate with gusto.

The widow was close to fainting by now for it was her fault that the whole town was flooding with gruel.

The girl, in the meantime, was unaware of all this, for the market was a good distance away and the gruel had not reached that far.

But she soon set off for home. Along the way she saw many people running in panic. "What is going on? Why is everyone running?" she shouted but no one answered her.

She soon saw for herself. Gruel was flowing down the street, straight at her, like a slow river. 'Oh my goodness! What's this?' she thought frightened. As she neared she saw, to her horror, that it was gruel. "Oh no! This has to be the pot's doing! I must rush home!"

She clambered onto a table she found floating. Using a stick as an oar she struggled to reach home. The moment she waded into her house her mother cried out, "Oh daughter! Where have you been? Do something, for it won't stop cooking!"

And the girl just went up to the pot and said "Stop, Pot" and the pot stopped instantly.

They all heaved a sigh of relief. But by now it was too late and the town was filled with gruel. However with this magical pot the girl helped the poor every day.

An Enchanted Bottle

An Irish Folk Tale

Mike Purcell was a poor farmer who lived not far from the Irish city of Cork. And no matter how much they toiled, his wife and he could not make enough money to feed all their children. Soon their luck turned worse and one by one all their animals fell sick and died until only one old cow remained.

"There's nothing left to do but sell the cow at the Cork fair," said the wife. "Or we shall be thrown off our land for we haven't paid the rent in a while."

And so the farmer took the cow and set off for Cork. He had walked quite a distance when he came across a dwarf.

"Greetings Mike Purcell!" smiled he.

"How do you know my name? For I am sure I don't know yours!" said Mike, surprised.

"Ah, I know a whole lot of things. Where are you going?" asked the dwarf.

The Enchanted Bottle

"To the market to sell my cow," replied Mike.

"Oh, sell her to me instead!" said the little man.

"And what'll you give me for her?" asked Mike eagerly.

The dwarf pulled out a bottle from his bag. "This bottle will be yours!"

Mike burst out laughing. "Have you gone mad? Why would I trade my cow for an old bottle?"

The dwarf said, "Do not be so quick in your mockery, Mike. This's a magic bottle and will make you rich!"

Mike still did not believe him. "Don't you want to be rich? This bottle can give you everything you ever dreamed of," the dwarf persisted.

Finally, Mike gave in and handed him the cow. Putting the bottle in his coat pocket, he said, "My wife is going to kill me for this poor trade but I shall take a chance."

More Folk Tales From Around The World

"When you get home place the bottle on a clean table and say, 'Bottle, bottle, do your duty!' and you shall witness a miracle!" said the dwarf before leaving.

And so Mike went home to his eager wife. "You're back early! Did you get a good price?"

"I got a bottle for the cow," he said. She was shocked. "Are you out of your mind? We're starving to death here and you sell our cow for a bottle?"

And she started to cry. "Don't cry my dear. This's a magic bottle. Let's at least see what it can do."

He set the bottle on a table and said "Bottle, Bottle, do your duty!"

And miracle of miracles! Two tiny fairies appeared from within the bottle. In an instant they covered the table with delicious food in gold and silver plates.

"Ah! Look at all this!" said the wife, awed.

They ate and drank with gusto and when it was all over, Mike took one of the plates

The Enchanted Bottle

and sold it in the market. Now they bought a horse and cart with the money. And then they bought more land and soon everyone in the village knew that Mike had suddenly become a rich man.

Their landlord was curious. "Tell me Mike, how did you become so rich?"

Though Mike refused to tell him at first, the landlord got it out of him somehow. "Sell me that bottle Mike and I shall give you a lot of money for it!" said he.

"No, no! I shall never part with the bottle!" said Mike.

But the landlord made him a better offer. "You can have my entire farm forever!"

'I would be very rich then,' thought Mike, 'And would never want any more money!' and so he agreed.

But he was wrong. Mike and his family kept spending money until they were poor once more. And again they were down to their last cow.

"There's nothing to do but to sell her," said the wife. And so Mike set off for Cork.

Just as he was thinking about the dwarf the little man himself appeared ! "I told you, you would get rich," said he.

"Well, I am rich no longer and I'd gladly sell this cow for another bottle," said Mike.

"Very well, here is another bottle," said the man and Mike went home happy.

Once more they placed the bottle on the table and said, "Bottle, Bottle, Do your duty"

And in a second the two big men came out of the bottle with big clubs in their hands. They hit the whole family until they all lay on the floor in pain. The two men then disappeared.

When Mike regained consciousness he ensured that his family was all right and then took the bottle to the landlord's house.

"Landlord! Look I've another bottle!"

"Is it as good as the first?" he asked.

"Oh much better," replied Mike.

The Enchanted Bottle

"Then come along in and let us show my guests for I am hosting a grand feast at the moment!" said the landlord.

And so Mike took his bottle in and placed it in the centre of the table and said "Bottle, Bottle, Do your duty"

In a jiffy the whole hall was filled with screams as the two men beat up everybody with their clubs.

"Stop, stop! Make them stop!" cried the landlord.

"Only if you give my old bottle back!" said Mike.

The landlord yelled for his servant to give it back to Mike. The minute Mike took the first bottle the two men jumped in and everyone was safe again.

Now Mike returned home and in due course of time he was a rich man again. They lived a very happy and contented life after that. And as for the two bottles two servants broke them during a squabble and no one could ever use them again.

Four Magic Bowls

An Indian Folk Tale

There was once a very poor couple who lived a miserable life. Every day the wife would nag the husband to find some kind of work.

"We are starving to death here and you do nothing!" complained she. And he'd wander around and return home with nothing.

One day she got tired of it. She scraped their pot of the stale rice that was in it and packed it in a dirty cloth. Thrusting it into her husband's hands she said, "Now, go and find work. Do not return home until you earn some money!"

And so the poor man set off and walked and walked till he reached the forest. Worn out, he decided to rest under a banyan tree.

'Some animal might eat my food,' he thought. So he climbed the tree and tied his bag of food to a branch. Then he lay down at the bottom and fell asleep.

More Folk Tales From Around The World

It so happened that the tree was home for some forest spirits. They were curious about his bundle of rice. "Let's see what is in it," said one.

They opened it and tasted the rice. "Oh, it is delicious," they cried. For they had never tasted stale food and it does have a distinct flavour. Soon they had eaten every morsel.

"We have eaten the poor man's food. Now, we must leave something for him," said one spirit.

And so they left four empty bowls in the bag and vanished. Soon the man awoke and was very hungry. 'I shall eat my rice now,' he thought and reached for his bundle.

But to his dismay, it just had four empty bowls! 'Curse the creature that ate my meagre meal and left these useless bowls to mock me!' he mentally scolded angrily.

And he banged the bowls together in irritation. No sooner had he done that than several beautiful nymphs appeared before

Four Magic Bowls

him. Each of them had a delicious bowl of food in her hands. They lovingly served him food. He was stunned but too hungry to question anything, He ate all he could. After he'd finished the women disappeared and the empty bowls were left behind.

He rushed back home and told his wife everything. She was thrilled beyond words. They kept the bowls in front of idols of God and worshipped them.

"It is God who has sent us this gift," said the wife.

Their fortunes turned after that. They always had good food to eat. One day the man decided to hold a feast. He invited everyone in the village. Many mocked him, thinking that such a poor man could hardly afford a feast.

But everyone went to his house and once they were all seated, the couple placed the bowls in the centre and prayed. Immediately, the lovely women appeared and served everyone with the most scrumptious meal they had ever tasted. More and more dishes arrived and the women served everyone graciously. Once everyone had eaten and drunk their fill, each thanked the couple and no one mocked them ever again.

There was one rich man in the village who was jealous. He pried the secret out of the poor man. 'Ah, That's easy, I shall take delicious food with me to the Banyan tree and surely I shall get an even better gift!' he thought greedily.

And so he had his cooks prepare the most wonderful dishes and the finest liquor and loaded everything onto his cart. He soon found the banyan tree and laying down all the food in beautiful plates and bowls he took a nap.

When he woke up all the food was gone and in its place were four empty bowls! 'Just as I thought! Who can resist the wonderful food I had set forth?' he thought gleefully, rushing back home.

Immediately he sent out invitations to all the rich people he knew, calling them for a

Four Magic Bowls

grand feast.

His guests soon arrived, mouths watering at the thought of all that food. When they were all seated, he took out his bowls with a grand gesture.

"Now bring forth the most marvellous feast for my guests!" he ordered. The next minute dozens of big, burly men appeared. They ran after everyone, pulling out sharp razors. They caught each guest and shaved their heads clean!

The terrified, wailing guests fled from the house. No one ever visited the greedy man's house again.

The Golden Shoes

A Scottish Folk Tale

In the Western Highlands, there stood a wonderful palace where a king lived with his baby daughter. The queen who had been a good and kind woman had died at childbirth. Soon the king married again so that his daughter would have a mother. The new Queen had another baby girl.

Although the stepmother was kind to the first little Princess, as she grew up to be a beautiful young woman, the new Queen grew jealous. "Stupid ungrateful wretch!" she would yell at the poor girl, and would beat her for small things. The king was away at war and so there was no one to help the Princess.

Every day she would go, sit in a field far from the palace and weep while sheep grazed around her. 'I wish I were a sheep – they are so much better off than I am!' she would think.

She made friends with one old grey-horned sheep. The sheep grew very fond of her and would bring her food everyday. If

not for him, she would have died of starvation because the Queen ensured that she wasn't fed at all.

The cruel Queen was puzzled. 'How is it that the girl does not waste away and die? She never gets any food,' she mused. 'I must find out.'

She sent a maid who was as wicked as she was to find out if someone was bringing the Princess food. The maid sent her daughter to the field to spy on her. Now this maid's daughter was sly and ugly and she had an unusual gift – an invisible eye at the back of her head!

She stayed with the Princess all day and although the latter grew so hungry she did not dare ask the sheep for food in case the maid's daughter would know.

Soon the daughter yawned widely. "Oh you look so tired. Come, rest on my lap for a while," called the Princess. The girl lay down on her lap and pretended to sleep.

But her invisible eye was watching. The

The Golden Shoes

Princess gestured to her sheep friend to come to her and he fetched her food. The wicked girl saw all this and when she went home, she told her mother all.

"My dear Queen, it's the grey-horned sheep that brings her food every day," said the maid to her mistress.

The Queen was furious. "Fetch the butcher and tell him to kill that sheep at once!" she ordered, "And ask him to bring back his flesh but leave behind the skin and bones. That should serve as a warning to the other sheep!"

As the butcher approached the sheep the Princess burst into tears. "Oh, it is all my fault! What have I done?" she sobbed.

The sheep comforted her. "Do not worry Princess, for I shall not die if you do what I say," said he. The Princess wiped her tears and listened.

"After the butcher goes away, gather my bones and roll them into my skin. I shall come back alive again!" said the sheep.

The butcher killed the sheep and took his flesh to the palace. Quickly the Princess gathered the bones and put them in the skin, but alas! She forgot the sheep's hooves! So when he came alive he was lame. But that didn't bother him at all and he continued to help her with food every day.

Days passed and the Princess grew even more pretty. One day a handsome Prince came riding along. 'Ah what a beautiful shepherdess!' he thought, enchanted by her looks. He asked the villagers about her and found out her whole story.

"Well, I'm going to marry her whether her stepmother likes it or not," he said, determined.

He would visit her every day and they were soon in love. When the Queen found out she immediately dragged the Princess back home, dressed her in rags and made her work in the palace kitchen!

Then she sent her own daughter to the fields every day hoping that the Prince would fall for her instead.

The Golden Shoes

The poor Princess was lonely in the kitchen and she sneaked out every evening to meet the Prince. One day he bought her a gift – the loveliest pair of golden shoes. And they were so tiny and dainty and fitted the Princess' feet perfectly.

The thrilled Princess forgot all about the passing of time and stayed out longer than before. When it grew dark, she suddenly cried, "Oh, I am so late! I shall be whipped for it!" and she ran.

In her haste she dropped one of her golden shoes. The Prince picked it up and kept it with him to return it the next day.

When morning dawned he made up his mind. "I shall go, seek my love and marry her. How long can this go on?" and he went to the palace.

He was taken to the Queen who was very impressed by his good looks. "What can we do for you, young Prince?" she asked.

"I have a golden shoe with me and I wish to marry whomsoever it fits to perfection," he declared.

The Queen thought quickly. "I shall help you find the girl you seek," and she asked him to wait. First she ran to the Princess and ordered her to get behind the fireplace and not to come out till called for.

Then, running to her daughter she thrust the shoe at her. "Put this on, quick!"

"Oh mother," said the girl, "This is too small for my foot! Only my stepsister has such small feet."

"Quiet girl! Stuff your foot in somehow! I don't care how!" barked the Queen.

But the foot simply would not go in. And so the foolish Queen called her maid and made her cut off her daughter's toes! The girl cried piteously but her mother said, "It's for your own good! Now come!"

And she took the girl whose feet were bleeding inside the shoe, to the Prince and said, "Here! I've found your bride!"

The Prince was stunned. 'This is not my shepherdess! I've promised to marry the one

The Golden Shoes

whom the shoe fits!' he thought dismayed. He had to agree to marry this girl.

The poor Prince tossed and turned all night while the Queen had already started preparations for their wedding. The next morning they were to wed.

The wedding day dawned bright and clear. As the couple walked down the aisle and the priest was about to begin the ceremony, a little bird sitting on the windowsill, cried, "There's blood in the shoe and the pretty foot is behind the fire!"

The Prince heard the bird. But the Queen hastily said, "Just ignore that lying creature and let's continue!"

But the Prince had to be sure. "I have to find out what the bird meant," he said and he searched the whole palace until he reached the kitchen. And there, behind the fireplace he found his beloved Princess.

"My love! I'd almost given up hope of seeing you ever again!" he said, embracing her.

The Queen was furious. Her daughter was relieved for she could finally take off the painful shoe. It was filled with blood as the bird had said. Servants cleaned and polished the shoe and brought it back for the Princess to wear. And of course, it slid easily into her foot.

"Come, my Princess. I shall take you away to my kingdom where you'll suffer no more!" and taking her hand he led her away from a life of hell.

They were soon married and the Princess always wore her pretty golden shoes.

Because of her greedy mother the innocent daughter had suffered.

The Kind-hearted Old Man

A Chinese folk tale

There once was an extremely rich man in China. Although he had everything that money could buy, he suffered an awful eye disease. He suffered greatly for he could not sleep in the nights.

"I've seen every single doctor and no one has been able to help me," he said, moaning in pain, "My wealth is of no use!"

Messengers were sent through the city offering a reward to anyone who could cure him.

Now, there was an old kind-hearted candy seller who lived in the same city. He was always poor because he kept giving away his candy.

He heard about the rich man's plight. 'Ah! I remember my mother telling me about a magical herb that's good for the eyes. Perhaps that'll help that poor man,' he thought.

Returning home, he told his wife his plan. "What? Are you mad? What'll we eat if you go off on your wild goose chase?" she said.

He left behind two baskets of candy. "I'll be back before these are over," he spoke stubbornly and set off.

He walked and walked until he was far from the city and deep into the woods. 'I remember how I used to spend all my time here as a boy,' he thought fondly.

As he sat down to rest by a stream, he noticed a large group of ants running helter-skelter. A rock has fallen into the water and the water had spilled into their nest.

'Oh no, you poor things!' he thought, 'I must help them for we are all one.'

He waded into the water and removed the rock. Taking a stick he dug a ditch so all the excess water flowed back into the stream. "There, your house is safe now," he said to the ants.

Then he found a shady tree and fell asleep under it. As he slept he had a dream that he was standing in the middle of a big city. A group of soldiers marched up to him. "Our Queen would like to see you," they said and

escorted him to a lovely palace. A lovely woman with a golden crown sat on a throne.

"You've saved us from the terrible flood. We're all one now. From now on, if you're ever in need, just ask me or any of my people to help you."

Said the old man, "Your majesty, I am looking for a herb to cure an eye ailment. Do you know where can I find it?"

"I haven't heard of it," said the queen in regret, "But keep looking and you shall find it."

And then the old man awoke with a start and realized it was the Queen of the Ants who had appeared in his dreams.

He continued on his journey, searching hard. He walked and walked until he got completely lost! Now, it started to get cold and dark. Finally too tired to walk any more he found an old, ruined temple and decided to rest in there.

As he entered the temple he noticed an unusual centipede! It had an orange skin with

The Kind-hearted Old Man

yellow dots on it and red fur in tufts along its back. It was scurrying as fast as it could towards the temple as there was a bird swooping down to eat it. The bird was almost successful when the old man waved his arms and shooed it away.

"You're safe now, lovely centipede," said the kind old man. He let the centipede climb onto his palm and took it with him inside. There he found some dry leaves and twigs and started a fire. Plucking some fresh leaves for his little friend he said, "At least, you don't have to go hungry tonight."

Then he lay down beside the fire and fell asleep. Suddenly, he heard footsteps near his head. Waking up with a start, he could only see the centipede. "Was that your footstep? I must be going mad," he said and closed his eyes.

"We're one, you and I," said a faint voice, "I shall help you find your magical herb."

The old man realized it was the centipede talking, but did not dare open his eyes. "Go south until you find a pine tree with two trunks. Near its roots there will be a magic bead. Dissolve it in wine and whoever drinks it shall be cured of eye disease."

'It is a magical centipede,' thought the old man and went back to sleep. When dawn broke he saw there was no sign of the centipede.

Eagerly he set off for the pine tree. He walked for such a long time that he almost gave up. But then just as he was about to turn back, he spotted a pine tree with two trunks. 'At last!' he thought and approached its roots.

But alas! His eyesight was poor and the ground was covered in pine needles. 'Oh, curse these old eyes. I cannot see any bead at all,, he thought, frustrated. As he fretted for a while he suddenly remembered the Queen Ant's promise.

"Ants, Ants. Come help this poor old man," he called.

Immediately, hundreds of thousands of ants started pouring out and stopped before him.

The Kind-hearted Old Man

The delighted old man said, "I'm looking for a tiny bead on the ground. Can you find it for me?"

And so the industrious ants scurried off, while he sat at a distance and waited. In a very short time the ants came back carrying a tiny bead with them. It was orange coloured with yellow eyes on the side. 'It may not look fancy but it has magical powers,' he thought putting it carefully in his pouch.

"Thank you, my friends, you've done me a great favour," he said and all the ants went back home.

Then the old man set off for home and somehow found his way back. The next morning he reached the rich man's house.

"I have a cure for the rich man's eyes," he said to the guard.

"You! Even the best doctors could not cure him and a ragged beggar like you will?" laughed the guard.

"Beggar or rich man, we are all one," said the old man.

More Folk Tales From Around The World

The rich man had overheard this from the balcony. "Send him up," he instructed the guard.

The old man went in.

"If you really have a cure for me I shall reward you. But if you are lying then you shall be beaten with a stick," said the rich man.

The old man produced his bead. "Dissolve this in wine and drink it and your eyes will be fine again," said he.

And so the rich man sent for wine and put the bead in it. After waiting for it to dissolve, he drank it all.

The next instant his pain vanished as if by magic! And soon after, his eyes were completely healed. He was delighted. "I'm sorry I misjudged you old man. I shall double the reward I promised!"

And so the old man and his family were never poor again and lived in comfort for the rest of their life.

A Little Warrior

A Japanese Folk Tale

In a small village in Japan, there lived a good man named Kenta and his wife Mori. They longed for a child and could think of little else.

Every morning the couple would go to the temple and pray to the Sun Goddess. "Oh, please bless us with a child!" they would plead, "Even if it is as short as our little finger!"

Months flew by and nothing happened. But one fine day, the woman gave her husband the wonderful news. "We're going to have a baby!"

But when a baby boy was born, to everyone's surprise he was no bigger than a little finger! Kenta and Mori were thrilled, nevertheless.

"The Sun Goddess answered our prayers," they said joyously. They named the little boy Issunboshi, which means 'as tiny as a finger'.

More Folk Tales From Around The World

The parents doted on Issunboshi and gave him everything he asked for. But though he never grew any bigger, he was very brave and strong.

One day he told his parents that it was time he made a life for himself. "I shall go to the capital of Kyoto and serve the king as a warrior in his army,' he declared.

Kenta and Mori were upset and scared for their little son, but realised that they could not stop him. And so Mori gave him a long sharp needle from her sewing box to serve as his sword. And Kenta got out a wooden bowl and chopsticks, which he used as a boat and oars to sail, to Kyoto.

Now Issunboshi bade goodbye and rowed away as his worried parents watched. And although there were strong currents, heavy winds and large fish, Issunboshi struggled along until he reached Kyoto.

'Ah, it is so beautiful!' he thought, awestruck, for he had never been to any city before. He now made his way to the palace.

Slipping through a gap in the gates he reached the king's court.

"Hello, great lord, hello," he said. But the king could not hear him for his voice was too weak.

He summoned up all his strength and shouted again. This time the king heard him faintly and caught sight of him. Picking him up in his hand he asked, "Who are you, little man?"

"I'm Issunboshi and I came here to be a great warrior of yours!" said the tiny boy.

The king was delighted at his bravery. "You shall be my daughter's personal guard then!" Issunboshi accepted gracefully.

Issunboshi started a wonderful life at the palace. The princess grew very fond of him and took him everywhere she went.

One day, the princess decided to visit a temple outside the city. On their way back, as they passed through a dense forest, a bandit jumped in their path.

A Little Warrior

"Ah a princess! I shall kidnap you and your father will pay a ransom for you!" he yelled, grabbing her sleeve.

She started to scream in fear and struggled to escape. By now the brave little bodyguard jumped down and headed for the bandit's feet. He took out his little sword and stabbed him in every sensitive spot he could – his toes, ankles, feet, heel – everywhere.

The bandit, unable to see him, hopped around trying to get away, but Issunboshi held on to his pants and kept stabbing him. Finally unable to take it any more the bandit ran into the forest, howling in pain. Issunboshi jumped down from his pant leg.

The princess cradled Issunboshi in her hands. "Oh, my brave soldier! You saved my life! Thank you!"

"Don't thank me princess, for that is my duty," replied little Issunboshi.

The bandit had left behind his bag in a hurry and in it were several precious stones

More Folk Tales From Around The World

and a mallet. "That is no ordinary mallet, Issunboshi. It's magical. Make a wish and it will come true," said the princess.

Issunboshi voiced the wish he had always wanted. "Please make me tall and strong like all other boys!" he shouted.

Instantly he became a tall, handsome and strong warrior! The princess was awed at what her tiny soldier had changed into.

The king was very pleased with Issunboshi. "You shall wed my daughter – she could find no better husband!" he declared.

So a great feast was prepared and the two were wed amidst wonderful celebrations. And then Issunboshi took his wife and went back to visit his thrilled parents.

Very soon Issunboshi became well known as one of the greatest warriors and kings of all times.

The Mermaid Who Loved Music

A Cornish Folk Tale

Along the coast of Cornwall lay the little village of Zennor. It was a lovely place with gentle waves and quaint houses.

The main livelihood of its people was fishing and at the end of each day, when the fishing boats had returned safely, the villagers would all head to the church and pray. And the choir would sing lovely songs, thanking the lord.

And in that choir sang a very handsome young boy named, Mathew. And not only was he good-looking, he also had the most wonderful voice in the village! His voice would soar above the other voices and every single note would ring pure and sweet. It was Mathew who always sang the last hymn of the day.

One evening as everyone was in church, the waves in the sea parted and the loveliest creature arose from within. It was a mermaid – half girl and half fish and her name was, Morveren. Climbing a rock, the mermaid who was the daughter of Llyr, the king of the ocean, sat down quietly to enjoy the sights around her.

As she ran a hand through her long hair, she heard the sweetest voice that the wind carried from the church. 'Oh my! Is that the music of the wind? It's so sweet and pure!' she thought, mesmerised. But then the wind stopped blowing she went back underwater.

The next evening she was back again and swam to the shore this time. Again she heard Mathew's voice. She sat still and listened, lost in another world. She had never heard such exquisite music in her life.

'I could sit here forever,' she thought, longingly, 'But alas! The water is falling back and I must go!'

She returned every evening to hear that angelic voice and her heart ached to see the person it belonged to. One day she pulled herself a little higher up on the shore and saw that it came from the church.

When she returned home that night she told her father what she had seen and heard.

The Mermaid Who Loved Music

"Oh, Father! How I long to see the owner of that voice!"

Her father frowned. "My dear Morveren, do not dream of going ashore for that voice. Hearing it is enough, do not aspire to see," he said wisely.

But she was adamant. "I must go father and see for myself. That music is magical and it draws me to it."

"It's no magic that you hear. It's a man's voice and we don't walk on the land of men," said the king.

But she became terribly sad until her father finally allowed her to go. "But cover your tail with a dress and return by high tide or you will be lost to us forever," he advised.

And so with great joy Morveren tucked her tail with a beautiful dress covered in pearls, sea jade and coral. Then she caught her long hair with a net and left for the shore.

When she reached the sand she had to drag herself up and crawl until she reached the trees. Then she pulled herself up and moved towards the church with great

The Mermaid Who Loved Music

difficulty. As she stood at the entrance of the church Mathew's voice floated out into her ears and captivated her. No one saw her as everyone faced the front of the church. So she stood in a trance, staring at the handsome youth who sang like a dream.

Every night Morveren would dress like a human and go to the church to hear the enchanting music. She would stay a few minutes and hurry away before the tide fell back. This went on for a year and Mathew grew even taller and stronger and more handsome.

One evening she was unable to take her eyes off him and she stood at the door longer than usual. And as he sang sweeter than ever, she sighed in happiness. And although it was only a sigh and no one else heard it, Mathew did.

And he looked up, his eyes fell on the stunning woman at the back of the church, whose hair had escaped from the net and fell in soft damp waves around her shoulders. Struck dumb by her beauty he stopped singing. That very instant he fell in love with her.

Morveren was horrified. 'I must rush. He has seen me!' she thought. And turned away quickly.

"Stop! Don't go!" cried Mathew. And he ran down the aisle after her.

As everyone turned to look, he ran out of the door and followed her. A mermaid could not really run and poor Morveren tripped and fell. But Mathew caught her before she hit the ground.

"You're the most beautiful girl I've ever seen! Please don't leave," he pleaded.

"Oh please let me go!" said Morveren tearfully, "I'm not human, I am a sea creature and I shall die if I remain here!"

Mathew saw the tip of her tail peeping out of her dress. But he did not care that she wasn't human.

"Then I shall go with you! I cannot live without you!" he cried.

And he picked her up in his arms and ran towards the sea. In the meantime the villagers

The Mermaid Who Loved Music

started chasing them, begging Mathew to stop.

"Mathew, don't go! Where are you going!" yelled his mother.

But Mathew, lost in love for the mermaid, did not hear them and ran faster.

As the villagers sped up as well, Morveren pulled pearls and stones from her dress and threw them on the road. Immediately greed overtook everything else and the men grabbed the stones.

Only Mathew's mother chased them till the oceans edge. By now it was low tide and was too shallow for the mermaid to swim. So Mathew waded deep into the water until the waters closed over them. His mother was left standing tearfully at the shore.

The two went to live in the underwater kingdom in a golden sand castle. And they were very happy together and were never seen by the villagers again. But Mathew's voice was heard as he sang beautiful songs for his beloved.

ಸಾಋ

The Miller Who Turned Into a Donkey

An Italian Folk Tale

Once a poor woman lived in a little Italian village with two children. When her husband died their lives became miserable and most of the time they went without food. Even their neighbours could not help them for they were poor too.

Weak and hungry though they were, the family always went to church to pray. One day she was alone in the church praying before the idol of St. Nicholas. "Oh Lord! Please deliver us from this wretched state!" she would pray.

Suddenly she heard a voice, "Go to the windmill and you shall find bread and shelter there."

Terrified, she looked around for the source of the voice but could see no one. 'It must be the prophecy of the saint!' she thought.

"But the miller is a miser – he'll never give us even a morsel!" she said timidly.

The Miller Who Turned Into A Donkey

"Don't worry about all that. Just go there and you shall be helped!" repeated the voice.

The woman felt it was useless to approach the miller, but she did as the voice bade.

She took her children and they walked towards the mill. Soon it started to rain very hard and they were soaked to the skin. The children started to cry from hunger and exhaustion.

Finally reaching the mill, they knocked on the door and waited outside shivering miserably. After a very long time the miller opened the door.

"What do you want?" yelled the miller, irritated at being disturbed.

"Please sir, we're tired and hungry. Can you give us something to eat?" said the woman.

"You stupid woman! Who do you think you are? Get out of here!" he shouted cruelly.

"Please sir, my children haven't eaten for

three days. At least give them some bread!" she pleaded.

"Take these urchins with you and go before I set the dogs on you!" quipped the nasty miller.

Suddenly, an old man appeared out of thin air. As the miller gaped at him, the man raised his staff and touched the miller on the shoulder.

Instantly the miller fell to the ground. As they all watched in fascination, he started to turn grey. Next, his ears grew long and pointed. His clothes dropped off and he sprouted a tail! He had become a donkey!

The children stared at him with their mouths open. "Eeeaaaaawwahhh" brayed the miller but he could do nothing.

"Go inside with your children," said the old man, who was actually Saint Nicholas. "There'll be warm food inside and soft beds. Once you're rested you shall take over the working of the mill."

"My lord! I don't know anything about the mill! How will I manage?" said the woman in panic.

"Do not worry. Tomorrow a helper will come here to work for you," assured the old man. "Remember to charge a fair price from your customers. And you can rent out the donkey if you like," he added with a twinkle in his eye.

Next he harnessed the donkey and led him into the barn. And then the old man disappeared as suddenly as he had materialised.

The three went in and saw to their utter amazement the most mouth-watering dishes in the kitchen. There was delicious pasta and big chunks of creamy cheese and fresh bread and what not! The starving family thanked the lord and gobbled down the food. It had been ages since they had eaten like this!

After they ate they found three wonderfully soft beds in the next room. Tired out after their long walk and the scrumptious

The Miller Who Turned Into A Donkey

meal, they lay down and were soon asleep.

The next morning a young man knocked on the door. "I've been sent to help you run the mill," said he.

"Welcome!" said the woman. And so he was hired and proved to be a hardworking and trustworthy lad.

A new life began. Every day the young man would harness the donkey and work him hard. With the evil miller gone, more customers came with grain to be ground. And even more came when they heard about her fair prices. Soon the mill was doing extremely well. And the family never went without a meal again.

One evening, after a year had passed, there was a knock on the door. It was the old man.

"Welcome lord," she said warmly, "Thanks to you, my children are clothed and well-fed."

"Come, let us see how the miller is," said the old man.

More Folk Tales From Around The World

They went to the barn where the donkey was tied up in a stall. The old man raised his staff and touched the animal. The next second the donkey's ears shrank, his tail disappeared and he became a man again!

"Well? Have you learned your lesson? Or would you like to be a donkey for some more time?" asked the old man, sternly.

The miller fell at his feet. "Oh no! I've reformed! I shall never again be miserly or wicked! I shall be good to people from now on!"

The old man smiled. "Very well then. Let this woman be your helper here and if you ever treat her badly I shall know. So, don't you dare try any tricks!"

But the miller had genuinely reformed. The woman and her children never lacked anything and the mill functioned well as before. When he grew old, he handed the mill over to the family and came to be known as the kindest man around.

The Paintbrush Phenomena

A Chinese Folk Tale

Ma Liang was a poor young man who looked after a rich man's cattle. Ma Liang loved to paint and he was constantly drawing and painting wherever he went. He would draw on sand, on the walls, on paper – everywhere.

One night when he was asleep he had a dream. An old man came up to him and said, "Ma Liang, I bring you a wonderful gift. Here's a magic paintbrush. Whatever you draw with it shall come to life! Use it wisely," and he disappeared.

Ma Liang awoke with a start. 'Oh it was only a dream,' he thought disappointed. But what was this? A lovely paintbrush lay beside him!

'Is this a magical paintbrush?' he thought excitedly. He immediately drew a cup of wine on the floor with it. Wonder of wonders! The next instant it became a real cup of wine. Sipping it, he thought happily, 'I can help so many people with this magic brush!'

The Paintbrush Phenomena

And from then he started helping as many people as he could. Once he saw some poor farmers despairing, for there was no water for their fields.

"I shall help you," he said and pulling out his brush, drew a river. The next instant the river came to life and the grateful farmers had water to irrigate their lands.

Another time he saw people struggling to till their lands and so he drew oxen. And when they came to life the overjoyed peasants could till their lands with ease.

Thus he helped several people and he enjoyed this greatly. He soon became the talk of the town. Shortly after, the rich man heard of his gift.

Summoning Ma Liang he said, "I hear you have a magic paint brush. Give it to me!"

But Ma Liang knew he was an evil man and refused. "It was given to me and I shall not part with it."

The rich man grew furious and ordered his servants to throw Ma Liang in the dungeon. He then searched Ma Liang's bag and found the brush.

'Ha, ha! Now I can get richer than ever!' he thought greedily.

He called his whole family and friends to his house to demonstrate the magical powers of the brush.

He first drew gold coins. But they remained just pictures! Angry, he drew jewels and precious stones. But they did not come to life either! In a frenzy, he drew a whole lot of pictures. But still everything remained as before.

He yelled for his servants to bring Ma Liang up. When he came up he said, "Quick, draw what I say or I shall have you beaten! If you obey I shall set you free!"

Ma Liang thought about it. 'This man is evil and I've to find a way to outwit him.'

"All right, I agree," he said aloud.

Pleased, the rich man said, "Draw me a mountain of gold!"

The Paintbrush Phenomena

Ma Liang put his brush to the canvas and started to draw a huge ocean.

"What are you doing? I asked for a mountain!" said the rich man, agitated.

But Ma Liang had finished the ocean and started drawing the mountain of gold at some distance from the ocean.

"Well, all right. Draw me a big ship so I can sail to the mountain!"

The ocean had come to life and so had the mountain. When the ship became real the rich man and some of his family and friends climbed aboard the vessel and set sail.

But Ma Liang was too clever for them. In a jiffy, he had drawn a monster wave. The wave grew bigger and bigger, approaching the ship at a high speed. Soon it engulfed the entire ship and everyone on board drowned!

Thus Ma Liang saved his own life and used the magic brush for many more years, helping scores of people.

೫ಌ

The Mountain Spirit

A Japanese Folk Tale

There was once a poor stonecutter who toiled hard to make both ends meet. He would trudge to the mountains every day and cut slabs from a huge rock for gravestones or houses.

This mountain was said to be the home of a spirit that granted wishes, but the stonecutter never believed it. One day he cut a large slab for the gravestone of a very rich man. When he went to deliver it, he was awestruck by the beautiful house the rich man had lived in.

'What splendour! I've never seen such riches!' he thought.

Every day seemed harder than before and he kept yearning for wealth. One day he was grumbling as he worked, "Oh, if only I were a rich man and could sleep in a soft bed with silk sheets!"

And a voice answered, "Your wish will come true – you'll be a rich man!"

Thinking it was his imagination, the man packed up and went home. But instead of his old hut, there stood a wonderful house! It was filled with lovely furniture and servants and, of course a huge bed with silken sheets!

He was ecstatic and soon settled down to a life of luxury. Days passed and summer arrived with a blazing sun. One morning the heat was so terrible that the man felt breathless and irritated. As he looked out of the window he saw a carriage pass by, drawn by horses and servants. In it sat a prince, looking untouched by the heat, a golden umbrella over his head.

Immediately the stonecutter exclaimed, "Oh, if only I were a prince so I could go out with a golden umbrella over my head and this wretched sun wouldn't bother me any more!"

And the voice of the mountain spirit said, "You shall be a prince!"

And he became a prince with the carriage and umbrella he wanted. He rode around in

The Mountain Spirit

style but soon realized that it was still hot. Even the water he poured on the grass dried up in an instant. He cried out in anger, "Oh, the sun burns up everything! He's the mightiest of them all - I wish I were the sun!"

"And you shall be the sun," answered the mountain spirit.

Instantly he was the sun and for a while he enjoyed shining down upon the world and burning up everything. He scorched the grass and burned the faces of men.

But how long would he burn things up? Soon a cloud passed over him and covered his rays and he yelled, "A cloud can block my rays – then it must be mightier than the sun! I wish I were a cloud!"

And then he was a cloud that sailed around blocking the sun's rays so that the earth grew green again. But he was soon discontented. He started to pour rain on rivers and streams until there was flood and destruction everywhere. Only one rock stood as it was.

More Folk Tales From Around The World

"Ah! But that great rock stands unmoved by all the rain! It's mightier than a cloud! I wish to be a rock!"

And so the voice answered, "And you shall be a rock" and he was.

He was happy for a while for the sun or rain could not harm him. 'This's the best!' he thought.

But his contentment was short-lived. For one fine day along came a stonecutter and started piercing the rock with his tools.

"A mere man is stronger than a rock! I wish to be a man then!"

The mountain spirit voice answered, "Your wish is fulfilled. You shall be a man!"

And so it was that he found himself to be a poor stonecutter once again. But there was one difference: he was happy with his hard bed and meagre food. He never asked for things he did not have, nor did he wish to be stronger than others. And he never heard the voice of the mountain spirit again.

The Two Bachelors And A Python

An African Folk Tale

Once upon a time in a little African village, there lived two men who were the last two bachelors left there.

There was Kalemeleme who was too timid and gentle to be heard and that's why he was still unmarried. And there was Kinku who was such an ill-tempered man that no girl in her right mind would even look at him. And they were lonely and unhappy and longed for a wife. 'Will I live the rest of my life all alone?' Kalemeleme would think.

'If only I had someone to cook and clean for me,' Kinku would think. One day, Kalemeleme took his bow and arrow and ventured into the forest for a hunt. Soon, he had shot a grey and a brown wild cat.

'At least I shall have a good meal today,' he hoped. On his way back home, he came across a great python named, Moma. He raised his bow and arrow to shoot it down. "Stop! Please don't kill me," said Moma, "Take pity on me and spare my life."

The Two Bachelors And A Python

Moved by its pleading, Kalemeleme lowered his bow. "Will you take me to the river where it is warm?" asked the python. And so Kalemeleme heaved the heavy snake onto his shoulder and walked down the river. Then he let him into the water.

"Thank you, Kalemeleme. You're indeed a kind man. Now throw the two cats in the water and you shall be rewarded by the water spirit," assured the snake.

Kalemeleme did as he was told. The water started to ripple. Soon it grew redder and redder until a big opening appeared on the surface. Kalemeleme put his hand in and pulled out a gourd (a vegetable).

'A gourd? Well I shall take it home and make a soup,' thought Kalemeleme.

And he took it home and cut it. The next instant the most beautiful girl he had ever seen stepped out of it. "I shall be your wife," she said shyly.

Kalemeleme couldn't believe his good fortune. And his wife was not only just a

More Folk Tales From Around The World

lovely woman, but had many other talents. She could weave mats and baskets, make pots, and was a wonderful cook and gardener. She always helped everyone in the village. Pretty soon the couple was the favourite in the village. 'I couldn't have asked for a better wife,' thought Kalemeleme.

Kinku was jealous. "Tell me Kalemeleme. How did you find a wife?" "The water spirit gave her to me,' said Kalemeleme. And told him about the cats he had thrown in.

'I want a wife too and I shall find one better than Kalemeleme's,' thought Kinku. With his bow and arrow he hunted and killed two cats – one brown and one grey. When he turned towards the river he too came across Moma.

"Don't shoot me please. Have mercy and throw me in the river for I'm dying with the heat," pleaded the python. "What do you think I am? You are a disgusting slimy python. I won't help you – you crawl to the river yourself," said Kinku. "Follow me, then," said Moma. When they reached the river Moma asked him to throw the cats in.

The Two Bachelors And A Python

Once he threw them in, the water grew red and an opening formed on the surface. When Kinku put his hand in up came a huge, heavy pumpkin.

'What on the earth will I do with this stupid vegetable,' he thought, grumbling. But he lifted it up and staggered home with it.

By the time he reached home, the pumpkin had become so heavy that he dropped it. The minute it split open, out stepped the fattest, most ugly woman he had ever seen. He was horrified. She boxed him on the ears. "I'm your wife, Kinku!" she said harshly. "Now bring me some hot water for a bath."

Kinku was very upset but was too afraid to disobey. And from then on he was bullied, abused, beaten and scolded all day. He had to cut firewood, he had to cook, he had to tend the garden – he had to do everything while his wife relaxed at home and got fatter than ever. 'Aarrgh! It is all the doing of that water spirit!' thought Kinku angrily. But it was his own fault for being nasty to the python.

The Woodcutter And His Enchanted Pitcher

An Indian Folk Tale

In a little village in India there lived a woodcutter named, Subha Datta and his family. And although they were poor they were very happy. Every day he would go to the forest near his hut and cut wood to sell to his neighbours. He had three little sons and two daughters and they would all help him.

One day he decided to go further into the forest to cut better wood. "Now, I shall be back soon, so do not worry about me," he said and left.

But he didn't come back for a very long time. What happened was this: He really went deep into the forest and started cutting down a tree. As he chopped, he suddenly spotted four beautiful beings. They were fairies, dancing round and round happily.

They caught sight of him at that moment. "Who are you and what are you doing in this part of the forest," they asked.

The Woodcutter And His Enchanted Pitcher

He told them. "You can't make money by cutting wood. If you stay here and work for us you shall never want anything ever again!" they said.

"But what about my wife and children?" he asked.

"We shall take good care of them, do not worry. They shall have food, clothing and everything else."

Datta decided to stay behind. He swept a clearing in the trees for the fairies and whiled away his time with them until they were all hungry.

"Let's eat now," they said and placed a big empty pitcher in the middle of the clearing.

"Where's the food?" asked Datta, puzzled.

The fairies laughed gaily. "Just dip your hand into the pitcher and ask for anything!" they said.

Datta put his hands in the pitcher and asked for rice, dhal and curry. In a trice there were delicious bowls of food in front of him! He had never eaten anything so wonderful in his life.

Time flew by and the fairies and Datta lived happily in the forest, eating from the enchanted pitcher whenever they liked and dancing and playing the rest of the day.

But soon he began to miss his family terribly and once had a dream that they were suffering without him. When he asked to leave the fairies said, "We don't like living with unhappy people. Go if you like."

But he couldn't bear to leave the magic pitcher. He stayed on for some more time.

In the meantime, his family had learned to live without him. His little sons climbed up trees and cut down small branches and sold them to the neighbours. The little girls also collected twigs and sold them. Taking pity on the brave children the neighbours ensured that they had plenty to eat.

Datta soon had another dream where his family was managing fine without him. He

decided to go back and show them how well he had done for himself.

He told the fairies. "We'd like to give you a parting gift," they said, for they had grown fond of him.

"I'd like the pitcher," he cried. The fairies were taken aback for they had no other means of eating.

"Ask for anything else!" they pleaded.

"No, no! It's only the pitcher that I want!"

They took him to their secret chambers and showed him precious stones and gold. But he still wanted only the pitcher.

And they finally gave in and he went home happily with the pitcher.

He had a joyous reunion with his family, but he never told them about the pitcher. He hid it in a hollow of a tree near his home.

Whenever it was time for a meal he would take a basket, fill it with food he got from the pitcher and return home. Although they asked

The Woodcutter And His Enchanted Pitcher

him several times he would never reveal his secret.

He became more and more proud. He stopped working and so did his family. Soon he started hosting wonderful parties for his neighbours and friends. The most wonderful food filled the tables and delicious wine flowed like water. Very shortly Datta started to drink too much wine. And when he was drunk he would say things that he did not mean to say.

One day his friends teased him. "You must be robbing some rich man to have so much delicious food in the house all the time!"

He became furious and under the influence of his wine he ran out and fetched his pitcher.

He pulled out more and more food from it and threw it on the ground. "Is this stealing? Tell me? Am I a thief?"

As he shouted he got more and more excited. Soon he picked up the pitcher and started dancing around wildly. "I can do anything with this magic pitcher, ha, ha, ha!" he laughed like a mad man.

His wife and children yelled at him to stop. "You're going to drop it. Don't jump around!"

But he continued to dance until he started to feel giddy and fell. The pitcher fell to the ground and broke into pieces.

Datta started to wail and knew he had only himself to blame. As he picked up the pieces to see if he could stick it together again, there was the sound of clapping hands and the voice of the fairies – "We have our pitcher back now!"

Now Datta mended his ways and went back to his old life. And soon they were as happy as they had been before.

When The Coyote Stole Fire

A Native American Folk Tale

A very, very long time ago, man did not know of the source of fire. In the summers he was perfectly happy but during the winters he was miserable. The chill froze him to the bone and many died because of the ice-cold weather and frost.

"Oh, if only I had a little piece of the sun to keep in my tepee" one of the men lamented.

Now the coyotes had no use for fire but there was one coyote who was moved by the plight of man. As he listened to the cries of women who had lost their loved ones to winter, he thought, 'I must do something to help them.'

The only place where there was fire was high up on a mountain where the three Fire Beings lived. They guarded their fire jealously, afraid that the man would steal some and become as strong as they were.

'I have to find a way to steal their fire,' thought the coyote. So he climbed to the top of the mountain and when he reached the camp of the Fire Beings, he hid behind the bushes.

"Who's that?" said one Fire Being, "Who goes there?" But when he saw it was only a coyote he ignored it.

The three then huddled around their warm fire and the coyote watched them all day. He watched them feeding the fire with dried branches and pine cones. He watched how they guarded the fire in turns during the night. One would watch the fire while the other two slept. Thus, they shared the watch.

'Hmm. It's during the wee hours that I must try,' thought the coyote. It was at this time that the fire was left unguarded for a few minutes. The Fire Being who had the last watch would enter the tent and yell for one of the others to take over. And that Being would be too sleepy to come out at once. Thus there was always a slack time.

And so the coyote bided his time. He returned to the village and told the chief of

When The Coyote Stole Fire

his plan. Then he returned to the camp. He waited all night. When morning came, the Fire Being on guard went inside the tent and yelled, "Wake up and take your turn now!"

"There's no need to yell, I'm going!" grumbled a sleepy Being from inside. But before he came out, the coyote pounced on the fire and grabbed a glowing portion of it.

As he sprang away down the mountain, the Fire Beings screamed and chased him. Suddenly one of the Beings caught up with him and grabbed his tail. But he could only reach the tip of the coyote's tail. That touch was enough to turn the fur white. And that is why coyote tails are white at the tips.

The coyote shouted out and flung the torch. The squirrel caught it and ran, with the Fire Beings after her now. She put it on her back and ran as fast as she could. But the fire was so hot that it scorched her back and her tail curled up. And that is why squirrel tails curl up the way they do till today.

The Squirrel then threw the fire to the chipmunk. As the chipmunk ran, one Fire

When The Coyote Stole Fire

Being clawed his back leaving behind three stripes. Even till today chipmunks with three stripes on their backs could be seen.

Unable to run faster, the chipmunk threw the fire to the frog. The Beings turned to him and grabbed his tail. As the frog gave a giant leap his tail snapped in the Being's hand. That's why frogs have no tails at all.

Now, the frog threw the fire to the wood and it swallowed the fire. The Fire Beings ran to the wood and tried hard to get it back. But they just couldn't. Finally they gave up and returned home.

But Coyote knew how to get fire out of wood. He spoke to the chief. "Rub two dry sticks together and spin a sharpened stick in a hole in another piece of wood," advised the chief.

And soon man had a wonderful warm fire and no one ever died during the winter months again. That's the story about how the coyote stole fire.